LOVE
KOMBUCHA

MAKE YOUR OWN NATURALLY HEALTHY DRINKS

MELANIE
MILLIN

PAVILION

CONTENTS

INTRODUCTION

My name is Melanie Millin and I am the Founder and Chief Brewer at Love Kombucha, which I founded with my partner in 2013. So far it's been an exciting and challenging journey. The more I learn about this fascinating drink, the more my thirst for knowledge grows. The capacity for new flavour combinations is almost endless and the longer I brew kombucha, the more obsessed by it I become.

Kombucha is an ancient drink made by fermenting tea and sugar with a live culture. As with other fermented foods, it is packed full of beneficial bacteria (that are great for digestion and gut health), amino acids and vitamins. It is naturally low in sugar and, whilst the brewing process can seem a little complex at first, it is really remarkably simple to make. You only need to spend about 20 minutes or so every couple of weeks to create your own wonderful flavours. If you're not sure about the level of commitment required, don't panic! Kombucha is very forgiving if you should forget about a batch or need to take a break to go on holiday.

Along the way (before going 'commercial') I probably made many of the mistakes that brewers the world over make, some of them harmless and others less so. I get regular emails from complete strangers looking for a culture to brew with or who have started brewing but don't really know how or why things need to be done a certain way. So – what better way to share some of this knowledge than to put it all in a book?

There has been huge growth in the popularity of kombucha over the last five years; and this really is a worldwide trend. Kombucha is already immensely popular in North America where it has stepped out of both traditional and trendy health stores and into the mainstream and shows no signs of stopping. Australia boasts kombucha fans in their thousands and there are some fantastic established brands there as well as reputable sources of cultures for homebrewing. It has always been popular in Scandinavia, Russia and parts of Eastern Europe and now Western Europe is grappling to catch up now that they realise what they have been missing!

So kombucha is a 'thing' that's not going away. Everyone I know thought I had finally lost the plot when I showed them this squishy, slimy 'gloop' and told them it makes a fizzy drink that is good for you and I was going to leave my job to start a company. But I was (and still am) utterly convinced that everyone should have kombucha (or some form of naturally fermented food) as an addition to their diet. I was so in love with this little glass

jar on my kitchen worktop and how it made me feel (we'll get onto that in a minute) that I genuinely just wanted to share it with everyone – without too much thought of the practicalities of running a manufacturing company.

From that point forth, I bored every person I met with all things kombucha. There were two overwhelming and consistent responses. Firstly, few people had heard of it – you might think that this would put me off, but strangely it had the opposite effect! If everyone knew of kombucha but chose not to buy or make it then I really would have been disheartened, but to me this seemed like the perfect opportunity to share the love I have for kombucha with a brand new and untapped audience. The second overwhelming response was genuine interest. I mean questions galore and encouragement that if it were commercially available, of good quality and at the right price, people would buy it.

Perhaps I was painting a particularly positive picture, based on my own good experience, but it's really not just marketing spiel. Let's put it in perspective: there's this drink that is very low in sugar, lightly fizzy and good for you. It is naturally packed full of bacteria and yeasts that are beneficial to our bodies and contains nothing artificial (no laboratory concocted

additions here!). It has a well-rounded, grown-up taste, not out of place in a wine glass or with dinner (how many soft drinks can say that?). Read that list again. And a third time just for good measure. Why would that NOT be a good idea?

So Love Kombucha was born. One glass brewing jar multiplied into two, which soon became a 25-litre brewing bucket. Quickly followed by two more, and three more and before we really knew it, Love Kombucha had a commercial warehouse with a microbrewery, a forklift truck and a license to operate it (still my most unexpected and favourite achievement to date!)

Slowly but surely, the kombucha word is spreading. I now have people writing to me to tell me that they are delighted they have discovered Love Kombucha, or that the blueberry flavour is their favourite. And to this day I am astonished that anyone has ever heard of us, let alone decided they have a favourite flavour! Nothing makes me happier than the anecdotes of real customers who tell us how it has helped them; from cutting down on fizzy drinks, or alcohol, to giving them a much needed boost during a period of illness, kombucha can be all sorts of things to all sorts of people.

It can be a functional, medicinal tonic that takes you a few minutes each week to make, or it can become a real hobby that you look forward to spending time on, creating something beneficial, completely from scratch. It can be as simple and quick as making a cup of tea or can become a much more elaborate process, as complicated as you want it to be.

HISTORY

Whilst Kombucha may be relatively new to you, it has, in fact been around for more than 2000 years and probably closer to 5000. There are many stories that claim to explain the heritage of kombucha, some of which are confused and others downright unlikely. However, the most widely believed is that the Chinese, in their quest for holistic health and long tea-steeped history, are the originators of kombucha. Written records date back to the Qin dynasty (220 BC) where it is referred to as the 'Tea of Immortality' and often the 'Elixir of Life'. Quite a claim! It is said that ancient emperors were sent off to war with a hipflask (or more likely an animal skin) of this bubbly fermented beverage to keep them strong and fit for battle.

Whatever the tall tales of the past, kombucha's relatively recent history can be more certain. By the 1900s, kombucha had made its way along the silk road from Asia and into Russia and parts of Eastern Europe where it became a staple in many homes. It was the kind of thing that would sit in a bowl or jar on the side in the kitchen at your grandmother's house and would be the first thing that she would reach for at the first sign of a sniffle. I have a Russian friend who is immediately transported back to her childhood whenever she smells the distinctive tang of a ripe kombucha ferment.

So what happened? Well, war happened, and tea and sugar became rationed in some parts of the world and hard to come by in others. As these are the two essential ingredients it is hardly surprising that this home production ceased to be a priority. Some households must have continued in order to keep the cultures alive and well (although you will find that they are much more hardy that you first expect) in order that they are still available today.

HEALTH BENEFITS

There hasn't been a great deal of investment in clinical studies on the health benefits of kombucha. The pharmaceutical industry doesn't stand to make any profit from the development of something that can be made relatively inexpensively in people's homes. There are, however, countless anecdotal accounts of people who have genuinely benefitted from incorporating kombucha and other naturally fermented foods into their diet.

Worryingly, a quick internet search will regurgitate that kombucha can cure every disease known to man, including the likes of AIDS and cancer. This is not the case! Kombucha doesn't 'cure' anything. However, it does naturally contain many of the beneficial acids that our own bodies produce to help keep us balanced and functioning well.

Many regular drinkers have noticed specific improvements in inflammatory conditions such as arthritis, gout and acne (thanks to the glucuronic acid which is a powerful detoxifier and helps in the repair of cartilage and connective tissues). Improved energy and reduced IBS symptoms are also noted (lactic acid increases the oxygen in the blood and helps balance the pH and well as encouraging the growth of beneficial bacteria in the gut). I suffered chronic IBS for about ten years – I always believed this was more stress-related than diet-related, however drinking kombucha has had a huge impact and my IBS symptoms have all but disappeared.

Kombucha also contains acetic acid (as found in vinegar) which naturally inhibits the growth of harmful bacteria and gives it its unique "tart" taste. We live in a world where on the whole, bacteria are frowned upon. We carry around antibacterial gels and hand sanitisers and are actively encouraged to use them frequently throughout the day. Our home cleaners 'kill 99.9% of bacteria'. Well what about the good guys? Not all bacteria are created equal and whilst there are some nasties that can make us ill, there are millions of bacteria that live (or used to, before we started killing them) in symbiosis with our bodies, whose job it is to help keep the bad guys under control. By incorporating kombucha into your diet, you are giving the good guys a chance to recolonise the gut. This can help with digestion and elimination (yes, that's a posh way of saying poop!).

There is now scientific focus on studying how our gut health (and more specifically the microbiome that lives within it) is connected to mood disorders (including depression, anxiety and even OCD), autism and Alzheimer's. Is it any wonder that all of these have been on the rise in the last 30 years, since we started introducing medicines and chemicals whose specific job it is to kill bacteria?

Nowadays, we are beginning to understand the importance of the gut on our wider health and wellbeing. We know that our gut is responsible for digestion, and we also know that if our digestion is out of kilter we can feel pretty run-down. The millions of living bacteria that are found in a good quality, unpasteurised kombucha are beneficial to our digestion.

HOW TO MAKE KOMBUCHA

So, lets get down to business. How do you actually brew kombucha? I often marvel at how complicated some people seem to make it, because the basis is very simple.

TEA + SUGAR + STARTER = KOMBUCHA

That's it!

No really, that is it.

Now there are some tips and tricks along the way and a few dos and don'ts but it always comes back to three main ingredients. I am a firm believer that you get out what you put in and, since we are dealing with an actual living thing here, it makes sense to use the best quality ingredients you can afford.

There are two methods for brewing kombucha: the batch brewing method and the continuous brewing method. We will start with batch brewing, which I recommend for those brewing for the first time. It is easier to get started in smallish quantities and stop at any time. But first, get familiar with the equipment and ingredients outlined here.

EQUIPMENT

There is no special equipment needed for brewing kombucha. You will find that you have most of the required tools already in your kitchen cupboards, so don't go rushing out to buy lots of new things. With the exception of a good-sized jar, make do with what you have at home to start with. Once you have brewed a few batches, you will have a better feel for what would make brewing more pleasurable for you.

YOU WILL NEED...

A glass jar with a wide neck that is big enough for you to comfortably get your hand into. I recommend a 2.5-litre (half gallon) jar as a good size to start with. It may sound like a lot of kombucha, but you won't be filling it up to the top, and you will also be keeping some of your finished brew back to use as starter for the next batch. Discard the lid – this is an aerobic brewing process, meaning it needs a supply of air in order to ferment. Kombucha also produces gasses as it ferments and these need to escape, so never put a lid on your jar as it will stop brewing (once the air supply is exhausted) and there is a chance that the jar can explode if it has a very tight seal.

A sieve or strainer Plastic or stainless steel are fine but avoid any other metals. This is for filtering out loose leaf tea (if used) and also for straining your finished kombucha before bottling.

A plastic spoon I use an old salad serving spoon with a long handle. Wooden spoons tend to split and can be difficult to keep clean, so plastic is a safer option (or stainless steel, but avoid other metals).

A heatproof jug or bowl I use a 1.5 litre/2¾ pint pyrex jug.

A piece of tight-weave, breathable material to cover the jar opening. Jersey T-shirt material is good as it has a slight stretch to it so you can see that there are no folds around the edge. Try holding it up to a window and if you can see through the holes then it's not tight enough. This is to keep out dust and, most importantly, fruit flies, who have a particular penchant for kombucha and like to lay their eggs on the surface of the SCOBY (see p.15) given half a chance. Muslin is NOT tight-weave enough and flies have been known to find their way through multiple layers of it.

Elastic bands or stretchy elastic ties to secure the cloth. I prefer stretchy, as you can be sure that there are no little folds in the side that a fruit fly could find their way through.

A WORD ON CLEANLINESS

Of course it is important to make sure that all of the equipment you will be using is clean before you start, including your own hands. But don't go overboard. Do not use any bleach, or kitchen cleaners containing bleach, or antibacterial agents on your equipment. Normal dish soap and elbow grease is more than sufficient and you must make sure that you rinse thoroughly. Wash your hands thoroughly, and then rinse, rinse and rinse again, making sure that no trace of soap is left on your hands. Traces of antibacterial agents will kill the culture, so this is key.

INGREDIENTS

Starter liquid This is some ready-brewed, unflavoured kombucha. Shop-bought is fine, just make sure it is unpasteurized. The purpose of the starter is twofold: first, you are introducing living microorganisms into your own brew where they can feast on the sweet tea; second, adding ready-brewed kombucha lowers the pH of your brew, making it more acidic and less likely to mould. Sweet, room temperature tea would go mouldy within a couple of days, so this is an important factor in protecting the brew until it is well on its way and producing its own beneficial acids.

Organic tea (green, black or white) Loose leaf or tea bags are both fine. I recommend using a tea that your SCOBY (see below) is familiar with, if you have access to this information. If the shop-bought starter says that it is made with green tea, then stick to green until you are up and running.

The tea you choose will have an impact on the base flavour of your kombucha. The most important thing is to select a 'proper' tea. It is common for anything that can be steeped in hot water to be marketed as a tea, but the culture used to make kombucha specifically needs the tannins that come from the Camellia Sinensis leaf. This is the plant that most 'proper' tea is made from. The tea that we buy as consumers only differs because of the way the leaf is dried. A white tea is the least oxidized and therefore remains the lightest in both colour and flavour; a black tea has been fully oxidized; a green tea is somewhere in the middle. The taste of your kombucha will relate directly to the tea; with white being the lightest, black the strongest flavour and green somewhere in the middle.

The Camellia Sinensis plant and resulting tea is considered a superfood in its own right, with high levels of antioxidants and metabolism-boosting properties. This powerhouse provides the SCOBY (see below) with high levels of the tannins, polyphenols and nitrogen that it requires to thrive, reproduce and convert into the beneficial organic compounds that we kombucha drinkers (and our bodies) crave.

Be aware that teas such as Earl Grey contain oils that can interfere with the culture and compromise its integrity. If you want to experiment with oils or other tea flavours, it is best to wait until you have some finished kombucha, and flavour it with a second ferment in the bottle (see p.62).

Organic unrefined cane sugar You can use other sugars and plain white sugar is what the culture usually finds easiest to digest, but as a fan of all things unprocessed, my cultures cope well with the unrefined version. Don't get hung up on the amount or type of sugar used – the sugar is not for you to consume, it is required by the culture to metabolise into acids. There will be a very small fraction of what you used to start with left in the finished product.

A SCOBY This stands for Symbiotic Culture of Bacteria and Yeast (see also p.15). You can buy one from a reputable supplier (see p.80), ask a brewing friend if they can spare one (anyone who has been brewing for any length of time will have spares and is usually happy to share), or you can grow your own. If you are buying one or being given one, it will come in some of its own liquid. Keep this to act as your starter liquid.

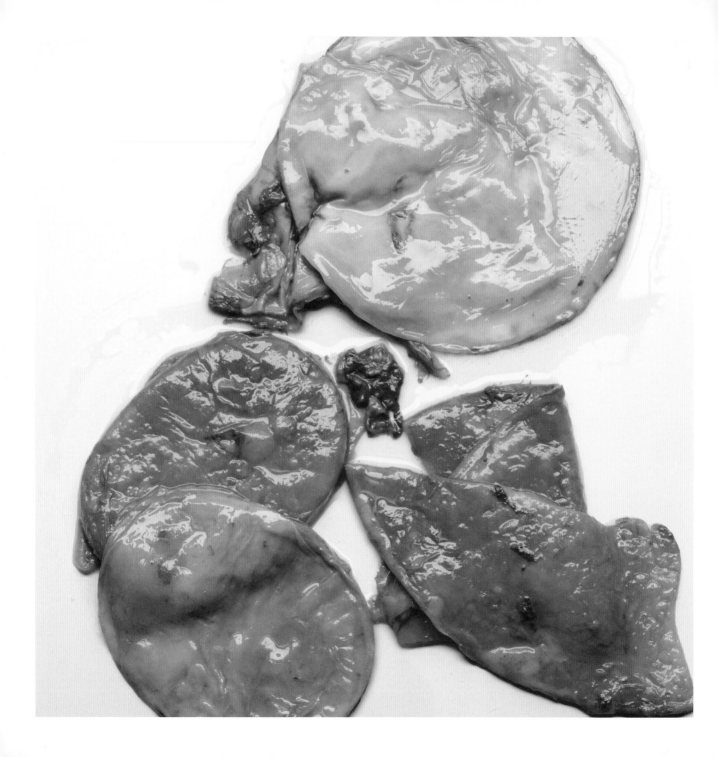

WHAT IS A SCOBY?

SCOBY is an acronym that stands for Symbiotic Culture of Bacteria and Yeast. It is the culture that transforms the sweet tea into kombucha. SCOBYs come in all sorts of shapes and sizes, depending on the shape of the vessel they were grown in, as they will always grow to cover the whole surface of the liquid. It is very common to see round or oval shaped cultures, but I have seen square and even hexagonal. If you are gifted one by a friend who has cut or torn a piece away from a larger 'mother' culture then it may be a completely irregular shape. All of these are fine. In all my years of brewing, the variance in the appearance of cultures never ceases to amaze me.

A SCOBY is a bi-product of the ferment. As you brew, a new layer of SCOBY will form on the surface helping to protect the liquid underneath. As you brew again and again, new layers will form, either attached to the existing SCOBY giving the impression of a thickening layer, or not, depending on whether the original SCOBY was floating at the surface or sitting lower down in the liquid (either is fine).

I have had smooth, creamy-looking ones, ones with holes in where the gasses escape, ones that look like they have warts all over the surface, thin paper-like ones (especially when there is change in atmospheric pressure) and old brown stringy ones – the older a SCOBY gets, the darker it will be in colour as it gets stained by the tea. This is completely normal and you can carry on using it indefinitely.

If you are feeling adventurous and want to grow your own, all you need is a bottle of shop-bought kombucha. Make sure it is unflavoured and unpasteurised – this information should be on the label. Pour the bottle of kombucha into your glass jar and cover it over with a tight-weave cloth, secured with an elastic tie. Leave in a reasonably warm place, out of direct sunlight, and the likelihood is that after a couple of weeks you will see a clear jelly-like film covering the surface. This is a new culture or SCOBY starting to grow. Depending on how warm it is, you may experience some evaporation. So, to increase your chances of growing a SCOBY from scratch, and to give the hungry kombucha something to feed upon, add a cup of sweet tea to the jar along with the bottle of unflavoured kombucha. Just make a normal cup of tea, with 1 tea bag or 1 teaspoon of loose leaf tea. Add about 2–3 teaspoons of sugar, stir well, and let it cool to room temperature before adding it to the jar.

Leave it alone for a couple of weeks and you will see the same film across the surface. SCOBYs don't always form evenly (or even smoothly) so don't panic. If it looks blotchy or thicker in some places, it is fine. Leave it to keep growing until it is at least 3–4mm/ ¼ inch thick, or thick enough that you can comfortably take it out of the jar and it will hold its form. SCOBYs by nature are wet and slimy and are plump with kombucha (if you ever see a dry or dehydrated one they lose most of their volume). If it is too thin, it is like trying to unfold a piece of clingfilm that has stuck to itself!

BASIC BATCH-BREWING METHOD

For a 2-litre/3½-pint batch brew:
2 litres/3½ pints filtered water
4–6 tea bags, or 4–6 tsp loose leaf tea
125g/4½ oz/⅔ cup unrefined organic sugar
200ml/7 fl oz/scant 1 cup starter liquid (see p.12)
1 SCOBY (see p.15)

So you have bought/been given/grown a SCOBY. Congratulations, you are ready to go! In your 2.5-litre jar, we are going to make 2 litres of kombucha. This is so that the surface of the brewing liquid sits at the widest part of the jar (and not up in the narrower neck) giving your kombucha the maximum available surface area with which to breathe, and upon which your culture can reproduce.

Use filtered water – a standard home filter jug or tap, if you have one, is fine. If you don't have one of these and aren't ready to invest in one yet, then a 2-litre bottle of water from the supermarket is fine. Boil 1 litre/1¾ pints of filtered water and allow it to cool to just below boiling point. No need to measure the actual temperature, but good quality tea leaves can be scorched by boiling water so just give it a couple of minutes after it has boiled before you use it.

For a 2-litre batch brew, use between 4 and 6 tea bags (if using loose leaf tea then 1 teaspoon of tea leaves replaces 1 teabag). This is down to personal preference – I use 6. Pour the hot water over the tea bags in the heatproof jug, stir, and allow to steep for 10–15 minutes. Remove the teabags or strain out the loose tea leaves and then add the sugar to the still hot tea. Stir until dissolved. Of course, quantities can be amended for smaller or larger batches (see batch advice on p.18).

Pour the rest of your plain filtered/bottled water into your jar, before adding the sweet tea solution. This instantly takes the heat out of the tea and stops the jar from cracking. Give it a stir and check the temperature with a clean finger. It should be at or just below body temperature. Any warmer and you will have to wait until it has cooled. If you are in a rush, you can add a couple of filtered ice cubes, but there is no harm in just waiting.

Once you are happy that the sweet tea is not too warm, then you can add your starter liquid. This should be around 10% of your total volume, so for 2 litres, you should add about 200ml of starter. I recommend that you have a taste at this point. It will be absolutely horrible! Sickly sweet and not nice to drink at all, but if you don't know what it tastes like to start with, how will you know if the taste is changing?

Add your SCOBY to the jar, cover with a cloth secured with elastic, and put it in a warm place out of direct sunlight. It may take a little trial and error to find the right place in your house. Windowsills are generally a bit cold, airing cupboards are too warm and lack airflow. Mine sit on the kitchen counter and seem very happy there.

The temptation, especially when starting out, can be to check on your kombucha daily, but the best

thing to do is to leave it undisturbed for a minimum of 7 days. I recommend brewing for a minimum of 14 days, and the longer you can go, the less sugar it will have and the more beneficial acids will have had a chance to form.

The brewing process is greatly affected by temperature so the cycle will vary depending on the time of year and the temperature of the room. The ideal temperature is between 21–27°C. If it is cooler, it will take a little longer, and if it is warmer, it is likely to take less time. Some people use heat mats or Christmas tree lights around the base of the jar to speed up the process and, whilst it will reach a sourness in a shorter timeframe, I am a firm believer that patience is key. It will get there in the end and your brew will contain a wider range of beneficial bacteria strains, yeasts and acid compounds if it is left to ferment in its own good time.

After 7 days you can start to taste. The easiest way is to use a straw and slide it down the side of the SCOBY. Once it is about an inch or so into the kombucha, just cover the end of the straw with your finger to create an airlock and pull the straw out. You will have an inch or so of liquid that is enough to taste how it is getting along. Kombucha goes through a tart phase between 7 and 14 days when most people would be tempted to say it is done, but actually if left for a little longer it tends to mellow a little more. The longer you can leave it the better.

Once you are happy with the taste you can progress to the second ferment (see p.22).

Batch ratios To increase or decrease the amount of kombucha you make, maintain the following ratio: 2–3 tea bags and 60–65 g/2½ oz/⅓ cup sugar and a minimum of 10% starter liquid per litre/1¾ pints. I wouldn't recommend trying to make anything less than 1 litre/1¾ pints, as you will always need to keep back some starter for the next batch and for storing any spare cultures (see p.20).

Putting kombucha on pause If you are away for 3 weeks or less, just make a fresh batch and leave it on your kitchen worktop. It will likely be too vinegary to drink by the time you get back, but the SCOBY will be fine and there are plenty of uses for vinegar (see p.73).

For longer breaks, store the SCOBY in some brewed kombucha in a jar with a secure cloth covering and keep somewhere out of direct sunlight. It can be kept indefinitely in this state, just check on it once in a while as it may need to be pushed down the jar if it is starting to rise up out of the liquid and get a little dry on top. You can also add some additional sweet tea, or brewed kombucha, if the liquid in the jar has started to evaporate. When you next come to brew, the liquid in the jar will serve as extra starter liquid.

Don't be tempted to refrigerate your SCOBY. Although it seems logical and some brewers have successfully used previously refrigerated SCOBYS, they can take several batches of brewing to come back to life and are much more susceptible to mould.

CONTINUOUS BREW METHOD

If you are getting a taste for kombucha brewing and find that your 2-litre jar just isn't enough, you can switch to a continuous brew. This requires a larger vessel with a spigot near the base. Once the initial batch is finished brewing, you can draw off between 10–25% of the brewed kombucha for bottling (that is ready to drink straight away or go on to the second ferment/flavouring stage) and replace whatever is drawn off with sweet tea. Because only a small portion of your remaining brew is new sweet tea, it is ready almost overnight. Also, as there is always a proportion of older brewed kombucha that stays in there you get the health benefits of a longer brew all the time, with readily available kombucha daily!

Make up sweetened tea in the usual ratios, perhaps just two lots to start with (you don't have to fill it up on the first go). I recommend transferring your whole existing 2 litres of brewed kombucha into the larger container as starter liquid.

SOURNESS / PH

If, in attempting to work out the right brewing cycle for you, you end up with a batch that is too sour to drink, don't panic! All is not lost. What you have is some really good starter for your next batch! If you want to try and drink it, then flavouring your sour kombucha with fruit and/or herbs can really mellow out the sourness. Alternatively, you can let it go even further until you have kombucha vinegar (see p.73)!

The joy of brewing kombucha for yourself is that you can have it exactly how you like it, however if you want to get a little more technical then another interesting way to monitor your kombucha is to check the pH. As the fermentation occurs, the pH will drop as the brew becomes more acidic. Don't worry, kombucha actually alkalizes within our digestive tract, which is a good thing. However it is the acidic pH which gives it a long shelf life once it is brewed. A finished kombucha should be at a pH of between 2.8–3.4 and can be easily checked with paper pH strips (make sure you get ones that measure the correct range), or even an electronic pH meter. You don't need to do this, but if it is of interest to you, it can help you to understand some of the cycles that are going on. Also note that the pH can meet the 'finished' range, but sometimes it can take a couple more days before the kombucha has the required 'tartness', so, as always, tasting is key.

NEW SCOBYS / SEPARATING SCOBYS

Once you have brewed a few batches of kombucha you will either have new, separate SCOBYs or your original one will be getting thicker and thicker. At some point you will need to separate a few layers or if you have one thick one, then cut a piece off. No need to throw them away, you can keep them in a cloth-covered jar with a little kombucha and pretty much forget about

them and they will be fine. Top them up with a cup of sweet tea every few months or if you notice that the liquid is starting to evaporate. Don't be tempted to put them in the fridge. Although this seems logical and will put them into a dormant state, refrigerated cultures tend to take a few batches to get going again and are much more susceptible to mould than ones that have been kept at room temperature in some starter liquid. They can be kept indefinitely in this state and you will often find that the holding jar itself will grow a new SCOBY as well!

Another reason to keep back-up SCOBYs is so that you can experiment. If you have an unquenchable longing to brew with Earl Grey or coffee (yes, it has been done!) then go ahead. Use one of your spare SCOBYs. Often these unconventional ferments work well for one or two cycles, but then the culture will expire, so have fun trying and always keep spares.

MOULD

The only true reason to ever ditch a whole batch of kombucha, SCOBY and all, is mould. Many an inexperienced brewer has mistaken new culture growth for mould and discarded a batch unnecessarily. Mould will ALWAYS look exactly like mould. Just like you would get on any other food – it will be dry and furry, with a blueish/greenish colour. It will grow on the top, dry part (not underneath). If it's not dry and furry, it's not mould and is likely new SCOBY growth or a fleck of tea leaf. If you are unsure, then watch it develop over the coming days. If it does turn to mould then unfortunately the whole batch needs to go. All equipment needs to be thoroughly cleaned and rinsed and start again. This is another great reason to keep your spare SCOBYs in a holding jar for backup!

ALCOHOL

We often associate the word 'fermented' with alcohol, and rightly so. In most ferments the sugars are turned to alcohol, however in kombucha brewing, they are converted into beneficial acids. There is a peak of alcohol in the brewing process in the early stages that may get as high as 2 or 3% but this is converted into acids as the brew progresses (another reason to brew as long as you can). As such the alcohol in your finished kombucha should be very low, at less than 0.5%.]

SECOND FERMENT (FLAVOURING AND CARBONATION)

Once your kombucha has reached a taste (and tartness) that you find agreeable, you can remove the SCOBY (if batch brewing) and pour it into bottles. (If you have progressed to the continuous brew method, see p.19.) It is ready to drink straight away if you wish. Many people enjoy their kombucha with no flavour added at all, and simply experiment with different base teas for subtlety. However, for many brewers, the flavouring, or second ferment, is where the fun (and fizz) comes in!

CHOOSING A BOTTLE

It is really important that you choose an appropriate bottle for your carbonation stage. There are hundreds upon hundreds of beautiful, decorative bottles available but as a general rule the prettier the bottle, the less suitable it is! Avoid square, hexagonal or other shaped glass, coloured glass (although standard amber or clear is a good choice), glass with moulded writing, or bottles that have any weaknesses (chips, cracks or air bubbles in the actual glass). You may think I am being over cautious but having an overactive bottle of kombucha shatter takes a LOT of clearing up. Believe me, I speak from experience! Sturdy swing-top bottles are the best and as they are designed to withstand pressure and can be easily found on ebay or home brewing sites or you can recycle your shop-bought kombucha bottles!

FLAVOUR AND CARBONATION

Provided you haven't heated it, your kombucha is very much alive and kicking and when you put it in an airtight container the living yeasts feed on whatever remaining sugar there is left in the drink and will create beautiful little bubbles that tingle on the tongue. If you haven't tasted a fermented fizz before, it is not the same as the large bubbles that you get in a standard force-carbonated drink, where the bubbles are large and gassy. Think of kombucha bubbles like fine champagne. However, you will need to get to know your own kombucha and tastes and, most importantly, have a little patience.

Kombucha is an aerobic brewing process, which means it needs to breathe. When we put it in an airtight container, it only has whatever air remains in the neck of the bottle or jar. Therefore at this point, you want to fill the bottle so not too much air remains. If using a slim-necked bottle similar to the ones shown, then you want to leave about 1 inch of headspace. If you leave more then it is likely that a new SCOBY will start to form as it carries on fermenting using the air in the bottle. The same will happen if your container is not quite air-tight. In this case the kombucha will continue to sour as the sugars are converted into acids. Rather we want the taste to stay the same and the carbonation increase, which is what we are looking for in the second fermentation.

The amount of carbonation you get and how long it takes to achieve it depends on a number of variables. Firstly, how much sugar there is left in your finished kombucha (this will vary greatly and you should brew according to your own taste preferences). It also depends on the container it is stored in, and the temperature it is stored at.

A reasonably good way of predicting what might happen is to bottle some with no flavour to start with. Store it at room temperature for a couple of days and then check it daily. Checking means opening the lid just a touch. If it hisses then there is some activity happening. If there is nothing, then switch to checking every two to three days. If still nothing then make sure it isn't somewhere cold and leave it for 7 days. Every time you open it, you are releasing the pressure build up, so if it is taking a while to build, then opening too often is counterproductive. You will soon get to know your own kombucha. If it hisses aggressively and bubbles up the neck of the bottle, then you are pretty much where you want to be (if you are looking for carbonation), and now is the time to refrigerate. Once you put your kombucha in the fridge, it will retain its fizz but any additional fermentation will slow to an almost stop. If your kombucha is too fizzy to open then make sure it is REALLY cold (in the fridge for 24 hours) and it should then calm enough to open safely.

My plain flavoured kombucha remains flat for months (although the chilly temperatures in the UK help somewhat). So, if yours isn't fizzing and the container is definitely airtight, then you can go ahead and flavour it without too much worry of explosions! I would recommend adding a maximum of 10% of the overall volume as flavour and leaving it at least a week before checking. Any more than 10% and your sugar content will start to creep up and you will override the tart taste that you chose when you stopped the brewing. Checking daily is counterproductive, as you will release the pressure which the kombucha needs to build up before it will carbonate.

A sweet kombucha in an airtight container in a warm environment can be a ticking time bomb! Yet adding flavour and getting the amount of fizz that is just perfect for you is all part of the fun. So you need to work out your kombucha's own character. If you like your kombucha slightly sweeter and with less of a bite (the joy of making your own is that you get to choose!) then it is likely that the finished brew has around 6–7g of sugar per 100ml and carbonation will happen quite quickly – within a week or so. If you prefer a more tart kombucha or want as little sugar as possible (for taste or health reasons) and so your brew has fermented for a little longer, then it will fizz, but will take a little longer – weeks, sometimes months. This is where the patience element comes into play!

If your first ferment gets fizzy in a couple of days, then you are going to need to be MUCH more vigilant when flavouring. I would still recommend that you don't go above 10% of volume for flavouring, as adding any sweetness at all is going to speed up the carbonation process. I would go as far as suggesting that you place your filled and flavoured kombucha bottles inside a shatter-proof container like a sturdy cardboard box or a cool box (not chilled), just in case.

Second ferment method So, once your kombucha has reached that stage where the taste is agreeable to you, you will want to stop it fermenting any further. With clean hands remove the SCOBY and rest it on a plate or other non-metallic container. During fruit fly season, be sure to cover it with a cloth or put a lid on straight away. Don't worry about brown stringy bits, these are just yeast strands and are an intrinsic part of the process. You can then pour your brewed kombucha straight into bottles or, if you prefer, you can strain it through a tea strainer or a couple of pieces of muslin cloth if you want to remove any remaining 'bits'. Be aware that filtering the kombucha won't stop further organic matter developing in the bottle, so it's handy to have a tea strainer on hand when finally serving. You can add your flavourings directly to the bottle in a variety of forms, as explained from p.26 onwards. A funnel is useful for decanting the kombucha into bottles if you don't want to spill the kombucha everywhere.

FLAVOUR COMBINATIONS

As kombucha has been around for so many years, it stands to reason that there are some tried and tested favourites that are made in people's kitchens the world over. Here, I will introduce you to some of the flavours that I have tried and loved, however, the sky really is the limit. If you have it in your kitchen cupboard or growing in your garden, you can add it to your kombucha and wait and see what happens! If you are feeling particularly adventurous, you can make your own reduction or syrup (see p.64) – just add a little at a time and wait a few days. If the flavour isn't as strong as you'd like then feel free to add more, but beware the carbonation.

Brewing kombucha is a relatively uncostly hobby. Flavouring your kombucha is the same. Personally, I like to juice my fruits (mostly because I am lazy and don't want to remember to have to fish out the pieces at a later date) but you really don't need a juicer to make beautiful flavours. Simply chopping, mashing or puréeing is perfectly adequate.

In all instances I would recommend that you source local, organic ingredients (where possible). You don't need large quantities so it doesn't have to be expensive. The only exception to this is honey. A raw, unpasteurised honey contains its own living enzymes that may compete with the micro-organisms contained in kombucha. If you want to use honey, then a standard supermarket variety is advised (most have been heat treated).

SAVOURY

When we talk about preferring your kombucha on the sweeter side, remember it's relative. Even a sweeter brewed kombucha will taste nowhere near as sweet as a fruit juice or almost any canned drink. So as its naturally not sweet (I wouldn't call it savoury but it has a quality not unlike wine, or even cheese), it is logical that the herbs and spices we use in savoury cooking, can also be added to kombucha to augment the flavour. Herbs and spices alone won't create a great deal of carbonation so, if that is your aim, then you will need to use them in conjunction with some other flavouring.

FRUITY

Fruit is a natural pairing with kombucha. Aside from the fact that most people agree that kombucha naturally has an apple-like taste, the sweetness of most fruits will help mellow the sharpness and help create fizz. Bear in mind that not all fruits are created equal – the sweeter and stickier the fruit (think mango or pineapple), the faster your kombucha will fizz.

GINGER

Plain ginger

Ginger & lime

Ginger & lemon

Ginger & peach

Ginger & star anise

Ginger goes with everything and is renowned for its health benefits, especially in digestion, so it makes absolute sense to boost kombucha's already pretty impressive super powers with the addition of ginger.

Something magical happens to ginger when it is mixed with kombucha. It is guaranteed to produce a great fizz, and so you'll often find a smidgeon of ginger with combinations you would otherwise not have considered. So, keep an open mind, even if you aren't a big fan of ginger generally. You can always reduce the amount you use and increase the other components if you prefer.

You can slice root ginger (no need to peel it) and add the slices directly into the bottle. This works well, and requires no special equipment, but it does mean you'll either need to scoop the pieces out once the flavour has developed to where you want it to be, or strain your kombucha through a sieve as you serve it.

Grating ginger also works well. The flavour develops more quickly than if you add slices, but you still need

to fish it out or strain it before serving. If you choose this option don't forget to grate it over a bowl to catch the juices and add all of this too.

By far my favourite method is to juice the ginger. Pure juiced root ginger is so zingy! Therefore you only need a very small amount. Juiced ginger separates into a murky brown water on top, and a much lighter layer at the bottom that almost resembles cornflour – this bottom bit is where all the zesty 'gingeryness' is, so be sure to stir or shake it together before adding to your kombucha so you get all the zingy goodness. Around 1% volume is a good starting point to give a slight zing and will help with the carbonation but not be overpowering. Therefore, to a 500ml bottle you would add 5ml, and to a litre you would add 10ml.

The same settling will happen once the ginger is in the bottle. Don't worry, your kombucha is still taking on that refreshing ginger flavour, but before you open it, you may need to gently swirl the bottle to distribute it evenly. Don't shake it! And if, for whatever reason, you forget this part... you won't forget it a second time!

BLUEBERRY

Plain blueberry

Blueberry & cinamon

Blueberry & ginger

Blueberry & raspberries

Blueberry & mango

Blueberry & lavender

With kombucha's already long list of superpowers, adding blueberry seems like a logical step. It is a superfood in its own right; high in antioxidants and vitamins K and C and relatively low in calories. Blueberries have the added bonus of giving the finished drink a beautiful dark purple hue. This deep vivid colour comes from the skin of the fruit, so make sure you include the skins.

You can just add the blueberries directly into the bottle and they will do their thing (they also look very pretty sitting on your kitchen worktop), although I recommend chopping them in half to help release the flavours and it makes them easier to get in and out of the bottle neck! The blueberries will gradually swell and turn pale as the colour leeches into the kombucha, you can then strain them out and throw them into a yoghurt or smoothie so as not to waste any goodness.

I prefer to juice the blueberries, skins and all. You will get a rich, dark purple liquid that can be added in and measured. Measurement is not particularly important, but you can record whether the flavour was to your liking and add more or less next time with more accuracy. This method also saves having to sieve out squishy swollen fruit at a later date.

With the shocking colour transformation, our preconditioned taste receptors anticipate that a bright pink/purple drink will taste sweet. It seems reasonable enough, but if you have only added blueberry, it produces a remarkably dry kombucha. I find it satisfies my craving for wine with food (come on, I know I'm not the only one!). Obviously it works well on its own, but if you want a satisfying fizz and don't have the patience to wait, then it can also be combined with a number of other flavours.

Ginger and mango are both well known for their carbonation qualities, so should be added with caution and checked regularly.

A stick of cinnamon can be added directly to the bottle. If you only have ground cinnamon, then grind it a little further in a pestle and mortar to ensure it is as fine as it possibly can be and then add a pinch at a time. Leave for a couple of days and then taste. You can always add a pinch more, but you can't take it away. The powder will sink to the bottom, but a gentle swirl will reawaken it and you will find that the flavour will still permeate the whole bottle.

Lavender has a very potent aroma and taste, so proceed with caution. Less is definitely more and a few lavender flowers will add a subtle complexity to the blueberry. This is a great choice if you are not so worried about fizz, but want a sophisticated flavour instead.

APPLE

Plain apple

Apple & cinnamon

Apple & cranberry

Apple & pear

Apple & ginger

Apple & mango

Apple & rosemary

If kombucha is likened to any alcoholic beverage, then most often it is cider. The yeasty aroma and sharpness on the tongue mean that adding apple seems like a natural next step. If you are feeling particularly lazy you can simply add some apple juice straight from a carton or dice a few pieces and pop them straight into the bottle. If using shop-bought juice, be aware of the additional sugar that can be contained in readymade juices and only add a small amount. If you are juicing at home I would suggest between 5–10% of the total volume, depending on how much patience you have waiting for the right level of carbonation and how much sugar is left in your brew.

To add rosemary, simply add a sprig or two directly to the bottle.

STRAWBERRY

Strawberry & basil

Strawberry & apple

Strawberry & lime

Strawberry & coriander

Strawberry, coriander & lime

Strawberry & mint

Strawberry & vanilla

Strawberry & rhubarb

Next time you've been to a 'pick your own' farm and have a glut of strawberries (or when they are sold as a buy one, get one free offer during Wimbledon week) fear not! The combination of kombucha flavours you can make with them is endless. You can make a fruit syrup (see p.64) or you can even chop and freeze them and pop them into your bottle straight from the freezer. When you strain them out later, use them in a smoothie or stir them into your yoghurt or morning muesli, so that the kombucha goodness they have become fat with doesn't go to waste.

As with other fruits where most of the vibrant colour is in the skins, they will pale (and eventually go white) as the acids in the kombucha steal their colour. Don't worry, this is normal. Strawberry kombucha is more of a reddish-brown hue than the bright red you may be expecting. You can minimise the fading by keeping them out of direct sunlight but don't worry if the colour pales, all the flavour will still be very much present.

When combining with herbs, I prefer to use a few fresh leaves or sprigs. Roll them gently in your hands to bruise them so that they release their flavour and aroma and pop them in.

Citrus fruits are pretty potent, so I would suggest that you are more reserved with your lime juice and just add small quantities. For a 500ml bottle, just 2 or 3ml is adequate.

Rhubarb can be added raw or if you prefer you can stew or roast it before adding. For more detailed information, see p.52.

MANGO

Plain mango

Mango & lime

Mango & watermelon

I have a bit of a love/hate relationship with mango kombucha. I personally don't like mangoes. I can cope with a slice or two but for me they are too sweet. However, my mother and grandmother love them! So, just for them, we launched a mango and lime kombucha a couple of summers ago (I had to have one flavour that the two most important ladies in my life could wax lyrical about when their friends asked, "so what is it like then, this kombucha?"). Many other people agreed that it was one of the tastiest flavours. What wasn't quite so tasty was having to redecorate my ceiling. Admittedly the bottle in question had been placed relatively near a radiator for about 12 months, but it took even me by surprise, so we decided that Mango and Lime Love Kombucha would have to be abandoned. However, you can still make it in your home, just be aware that the natural sweetness of the mango or mango juice is what gets the living yeasts excited, and they are what create the fizz. As a general rule, the sweeter the juice or fruit added for a second ferment in the bottle, the faster and more effervescent the carbonation will be.

If you are a fan of the taste of mango, this one is guaranteed to tickle your taste buds and you definitely don't need to keep it for a year. In fact I'd be surprised if it lasts more than a week! Once the carbonation is where you like it, just pop it in the fridge to chill. Especially refreshing on a warm day.

As with other fruits, you can simply cut some chunks and pop them into the bottle. The colour of your kombucha won't change significantly, as the colour is in the flesh rather then the skin (which has a bitter taste so you should peel and discard). Just strain when serving and you can eat or add to a smoothie.

If you want your kombucha to take on some of the orange colour and aren't a fan of booch-soaked fruit, then you can juice your mango first. It will settle to the bottom of the bottle but an occasional (and gentle) turn upside down and back again is all that is needed to mix it back in and distribute the slightly denser juice throughout the bottle.

ORANGE

Plain orange

Orange & ginger

Orange & vanilla

Orange & mint

Orange & cranberry

Orange & pineapple

Orange is a versatile citrus fruit and pairs well with many other flavours. A vitamin powerhouse with polyphenols, soluble fibre and plenty of vitamin C, to add it to your kombucha is to boost both the flavour and the health benefits. Readily available both fresh and pre-juiced, it is also a convenient ingredient that you are likely to have already in your kitchen. Oranges are another example (along with lemons and kombucha itself), of foods that are acidic before you digest them, but contain many alkaline minerals that help to balance out the body after they are digested.

As with other citrus fruits, you will only need to add a small amount to your kombucha. Start with around 10ml in a 500ml bottle and leave it to mature for a few days before tasting. As with all second ferments, the sharpness will mellow and the carbonation will begin, so you will be able to see whether 10ml will be enough for your personal tastes.

If you are adding complimentary vanilla or mint, you can keep the same amount of orange per bottle. When you are adding another strong flavour, such as pineapple or ginger, halve the quantities to 5ml of each, as both pineapple and ginger are renowned for creating their own fizz. You can always add a little more, which is preferable to losing most of the bottle in fizz, if you add too much to start with!

WATERMELON

Plain watermelon

Watermelon & mint

Watermelon, mint & cucumber

Watermelon is one of my absolute favourite things with which to flavour kombucha. It can be juiced or sliced and gives a really clean refreshing taste. The colour is a beautiful subtle pinky red and it gives a good fizz in a relatively short space of time.

You want to add around 4 'fingers' of watermelon to a 500ml bottle, or around 50ml of juice.

I prefer not to 'muddy' the freshness of watermelon with other fruits, although feel free to experiment with your own combinations. Other 'clean' tastes that work well are mint and cucumber. Just a sprig of mint is all you need and this can be added directly to the bottle. Cucumber can be juiced or sliced and added.

You will find that both the mint and cucumber will begin to look rather anaemic after a few days, so if you want to garnish the glass when you serve then keep some fresh mint in reserve for this.

Serve through a tea strainer to catch the pale cucumber and mint. These can then be added to a smoothie as they will have absorbed much of the kombucha goodness and flavour.

PINEAPPLE

Plain pineapple

Pineapple & mint

Pineapple & rosemary

Pineapple & coriander

Pineapple is a nutritional powerhouse whose benefits far outweigh the potential negative of its relatively high sugar content. They are high in vitamin C, manganese, which is beneficial for bone density, and bromelain, which is excellent for fighting inflammation.

The natural sweetness means that, much like mango, adding pineapple to your brew is guaranteed to produce a great carbonation. It is better to be conservative with how much pineapple juice or fruit you add to begin with, unless you fancy some spontaneous ceiling redecoration. If adding juice, stick to around 10–20 ml in a 500ml bottle. If adding fruit chunks, use half of what you normally would. This is one of the reasons I prefer to combine it with herbs than with other fruits.

Pineapple works well with mint, coriander or rosemary. For each, just one sprig is enough. Roll the herbs gently between the palms of your hands to release the oils (and aroma) before adding directly to the bottle. The herbs will quickly lose their colour in the acidic environment of your kombucha, so keep some fresh herbs back to garnish when serving.

Because of the guaranteed fizz, I recommend that you shorten the time you store your bottle at room temperature. If you would normally leave your kombucha around seven days to get a good fizz, then start checking after about four days.

POMEGRANATE

Plain pomegranate

Pomegranate & mint

Pomegranate & cucumber

Pomegranate & lemon or lime

If you are trying to entice someone to try kombucha for the first time, but they have been put off by the alien-like creature in the jar on your kitchen worktop, then pomegranate is a great place to start. The little pillows of bright colour look fantastic in the bottle and, as you aren't processing them in any way, all of the beneficial polyphenols, tannins and acids remain intact and will transfer into your finished kombucha.

Break out the juicy seeds into a bowl (this is a little messy, but it is also part of the fun and a great way to get children involved in making up their favourite flavours). Mash around half of the seeds with the back of a fork to release some of the juice and spoon the seeds into the bottle. I use a children's medicine dispensing syringe to suck the juice from the bottom of the bowl and put straight into the neck of the bottle. I haven't yet found another device as well suited to this task.

The bruised or mashed seeds will lose all of their colour to the kombucha over the coming days and the ones that weren't mashed will keep most of theirs so you end up with an array of white and pink seeds suspended in the pink kombucha.

Pomegranate is great on its own but you can spice it up with a squeeze of lemon or lime for extra zing.

Cucumber and mint are also great with pomegranate kombucha, although I prefer to add a sprig and a couple of thin slices of cucumber to the glass when serving.

CUCUMBER & MINT

Cucumber and mint is a good option if you want your kombucha subtley flavoured but not too fizzy. It is particularly palate cleansing and the mint adds an extra freshness. This combination stands alone or mixes well with other fruits.

PEAR

A ripe pear will yield a good amount of juice which can be added straight to the bottle (no more than about 10% of the total volume or it will fizz too much and be difficult to open). It won't give much colour but a lovely sweetness. It mixes well with most other fruits. Lemon, apple and ginger are all good pear-ings!

Pears naturally contain a good amount of soluble fibre and vitamins C, K and B2, B3 and B6 – so they make a great addition to an already healthy drink.

Pear is another good option to sweeten to suit a child's tastebuds. For this I would suggest a plain kombucha mixed half and half with pear juice directly in the glass and served immediately.

GRAPE

Grape juice is a firm favourite on its own! Pure grape juice is very sweet, so if you are after a very low sugar option then this might not be for you. However, it is also one of the most delicious flavours of kombucha you can make and many of the experienced kombucha brewers have this on the absolute top of their favourites list. Perhaps that is partly because of the great fizz it produces, so a word of caution until you have familiarised yourself with your own particular kombucha and how it behaves in a second ferment. Stick to a maximum of 10% grape juice and check daily until you get a feel for how it is getting along.

PEACH

Peaches are high in antioxidants and minerals such as iron, fluoride and potassium. They are also delicious added to kombucha for a second ferment! Peach goes very well with ginger for a great fizz.

cucumber and mint

pear

grape

peach

RHUBARB

Plain rhubarb

Rhubarb & honey

Rhubarb & apricot

Rhubarb & ginger

Rhubarb & peach

Rhubarb & plum

As I was growing up, rhubarb always seemed very old-fashioned. Perhaps it was that the old folk in my family seemed to like rhubarb crumble (I have since also acquired this taste) or that it was a slimy ingredient in anaemic-looking school puddings. However in recent years, I suppose thanks to the endorsement of celebrity chefs, rhubarb sales have sky rocketed! It is low GI and has been credited with reducing cholesterol.

Rhubarb on its own has a tartness that almost matches kombucha itself! There are a number of ways we can help bring out the flavour so that it will have the carbonating effect we are looking for in a second ferment. In some health shops you can now pick up rhubarb 'bites' which are pieces soaked in apple juice and then dehydrated. These can be added directly into the bottle on their own or with a squeeze of honey to create a complex flavour with an excellent fizz.

You can also make a rhubarb syrup using the basic syrup technique on p.64, which will intensify the flavour of rhubarb without confusing it with other flavours too much

If you don't want to add too much sugar then pairing rhubarb with a sweeter fruit will give enough sweetness to activate the yeasts to carbonate, whist still getting the tartness of rhubarb.

ALMOND EXTRACT

Almond & cherry

Almond & pear

There is no reason to stick to just fruit or spices to flavour your kombucha. Extracts such as almond or vanilla also work well and are relatively inexpensive. They also open up a world of other flavour combinations.

Almond and fresh cherries is one of the best. The sweet/tart cherries are a little fiddly with their stones but well worth the bother of de-stoning. Use them skins and all for maximum colour impact and add them directly into the bottle. Add around a quarter of a teaspoon of almond extract to a 500ml bottle to start with. Remember an extract is much more potent and you can always add more. Give the bottle a shake to combine but don't worry if the extract pools like an oil on the surface, it will still flavour the kombucha. The extracts alone won't create much fizz so if that is what you are trying to achieve then you will need to add a little something else. Raisins are a good addition to help with fizz but without adding too much flavour to spoil the taste of the pure extract.

CHIA SEEDS (WITH BLUEBERRY)

These minute little grains are packed with so many nutrients that they are among healthiest foods on the planet. They are low in carbohydrates and high in fibre. They are high in antioxidants, protein and omega-3 fatty acids. In fact they are even higher in omega-3 fatty acids than salmon! They are said to lower the risk of heart disease and type 2 diabetes. They are also good for bone health as they contain calcium, phosphorus and magnesium.

You have to admit, it is rather an impressive list.

They also don't really taste of anything at all so you can sneak them into all sorts of things (I have been known to add a few tablespoons into my family's spaghetti bolognese and none of them were any the wiser!)

To add them to kombucha, you need to hydrate them first. Add 1 part chia seeds to 4 parts warm water. Stir and allow them to sit and cool. You can rest them overnight in the fridge if you prefer. The seeds will swell to about ten times their original size and will be surrounded by a viscous jelly – don't panic, this is normal.

I like to add them to a blueberry kombucha to create a real antioxidant powerhouse. They will suspend in the bottle or glass giving them an almost hypnotic quality. I have caught my seven year old turning the bottle around and around whilst staring at it like a snow globe or lava lamp.

Surprisingly, chia seeds contribute to a good amount of carbonation, so if you want to add them to an already fizzy flavour then just serve them in the glass.

They can be added to any flavour, but if colourless (plain), they aren't nearly as striking.

GOJI BERRIES

These shrivelled red berries are alleged to boost the immune system and brain activity, protect against heart disease and cancer, and improve life expectancy. Goji berries contain vitamin C, vitamin B2, vitamin A, iron, selenium and other antioxidants. They have been used for thousands of years in the Far East by herbalists and produce a delicious lightly flavoured kombucha packed full of the combination of kombucha and goji berry benefits.

You can of course combine goji berries with other fruits, but they work well on their own also. They are slightly sweet and usually come dried so can be a little crunchy. Unlike some berries, they don't need to be pierced or chopped before adding to your kombucha. Just pop them into your bottle of plain brewed kombucha. Some will float and some will sink, but over the coming days as they rehydrate with the kombucha, they will rise to the surface and turn the kombucha itself a pale orange colour. Serve through a strainer if you want to save the berries for a smoothie or they are perfect for stirring into a yoghurt or porridge.

SPINACH, KIWI & WATERCRESS

These are three of my favourite ingredients for my morning supergreen juice (usually along with cucumber, celery and an apple) so I wanted to experiment with supercharging my kombucha with something similar.

The spinach gives a really deep, dark green with its high iron content and impressive list of vitamins K, A, C and folic acid.

Watercress adds a peppery spiciness and has vitamins B1, B2, B6, C, E, manganese, carotene, calcium, soluble fibre, iron and copper in abundance.

All of this leafy greenness needs balancing with some fruit, and kiwi has the perfect balance of sharp and sweet. It is also said to be excellent for maintaining skin tone and texture, reducing blood pressure and preventing heart disease.

To get the vivid green, you will need to juice all of the ingredients and add directly to the bottle (with the tried and tested children's medicine dispenser!). The slightly more dense green juice will separate and float to the top to start with. For the most vivid colour, drink within the first few days. If you are less worried about the colour then you can leave it to infuse and mature for a longer period of time.

HERBS, SPICES & FLOWERS

Plain lavender

Lavender & chamomile

Lavender & honey

Tumeric & ginger

Rosewater

If you genuinely don't have a sweet tooth at all, or need to keep your fructose consumption to an absolute minimum, then herbs and flowers can add an earthy or aromatic dimension to your finished kombucha.

Turmeric root can be diced or juiced and added much like ginger. The fresh root can be hard to come by, so it is fine to use the more commonly available turmeric powder instead. You should grind the powder in a pestle and mortar to make sure it is fine as you can make it as it does have a tendency to sink to the bottom of the bottle. Even when it sinks, it only takes a gentle swirl to mix it back in and the flavour will still permeate the kombucha evenly.

Lavender is particularly aromatic. It is fairly potent and you will only need to add one sprig to the bottle. You can strip the flowers from the sprig and add them separately if you prefer, but they are likely to float on the surface rather than infuse, as they will if submerged with the stalk.

Lavender pairs well with honey. Add a shop bought honey rather than a local raw honey so that the natural microbes don't battle with the kombucha. Honey will sink and look like it doesn't want to mix, but it will. Be sure to persist until the honey combines with the kombucha when it is added, rather than be vigorous with it once it has been sat for a few days as you risk agitating it so that it is too fizzy to open.

The easiest way to add chamomile is to empty the contents of a plain chamomile tea bag directly into the bottle. Over the coming days it will infuse but the flavour is delicate, so the longer you can leave the kombucha to ferment the better.

Rosewater is another subtle addition that can bring a depth and fragrant complexity to your finished kombucha. These delicacies are best combined with a lighter kombucha brewed purely with green or white tea rather than the stronger black variety.

TEA FLAVOURS

As tea becomes an increasingly popular beverage, there are ever growing numbers of 'tea' varieties available. In this instance I am referring to anything that comes in a tea bag and not specifically originating from the camellia sinensis plant, although of course it can do.

Although the very basis for kombucha is tea, the finished product doesn't really have much tea left in it and certainly doesn't taste of it, therefore adding the tea flavour back in is perfectly acceptable. It will take quite a while for the kombucha to take on the tea flavour as you are effectively cold brewing if you just add the bag or the leaves directly to the kombucha. You could gently warm the kombucha to around body temperature which is warm enough to begin releasing the flavour from the tea bag more effectively whilst not killing the kombucha itself.

Some of the fruity 'tea' flavours have great colour and will quickly and dramatically change the colour of your kombucha whilst adding a subtle flavour. Don't be afraid of breaking open the tea bag and pouring the contents directly into the bottle. This can be strained out using a small tea strainer when you drink the kombucha at a later date. The longer the leaves stay in there, the greater the intensity of flavour will be.

SYRUP REDUCTIONS

Fruit syrups are ridiculously easy to make, and serve endless purposes. The combination of the added sugar and the concentrated fruit flavours mean they are an excellent addition to your kombucha and are guaranteed to generate good carbonation in the bottle.

You can use almost any fruit you can think of. If you are baking pies, save your apple or pear peelings and cores for syrup-making.

Here's how to do it: add 4 parts fruit : 2 parts sugar : 1 part water into a pot. Simmer for a good long while, until the fruit is softened to the point of collapse. Strain out the fruit, and keep the liquid. You can store it in the fridge for up to 7 days.

Be creative and customize your syrups. Fresh herbs are your friend – thyme, basil, and bay leaves pair well with fruit. The same goes for spices. The addition of a pinch of cinnamon and nutmeg to your syrup will yield a warming kombucha to remember. Citrus syrups, perhaps more than other fruit flavour, are well suited to both sweet and savoury combinations.

COCKTAILS & MOCKTAILS

I have lost count of the number of first-time kombucha tasters who ask whether it is alcoholic. The yeasty fermented aroma is definitely one that we associate with booze. Most usually call it a 'grown up' taste. This combination makes it an ideal alcohol replacement. Of course it can be enjoyed on its own and isn't out of place in a wine glass at the dinner table. But why not give yourself a real treat and mix yourself up a cocktail (or mocktail for the tee-totallers).

Kombucha makes an excellent healthy mixer. The sharp taste and fizz mimic many drinks that we would usually combine with spirits and tend to compliment their accompaniment rather than smother them. My all-time favorite is ginger and lime kombucha mixed with gin, so simple and just perfect.

For the more adventurous among us, kombucha makes a perfect cocktail ingredient. Before refrigerated transport was available, citrus fruit was not easily shipped around the world so people actually used vinegar to balance the sweetness of their cocktails. I tend to gravitate towards citrus flavoured kombucha for cocktails, but you can really let your imagination run wild. Here are a few ideas for starters.

FROZEN KOMBUCHA MARGARITA

Serves 1
150ml/5 fl oz ginger kombucha (see p.29)
50ml/1½ fl oz lime juice
1 tsp golden syrup or maple syrup
50ml/1½ fl oz good quality tequila
handful of ice cubes
lime slices to garnish
sea salt for the rim of the glass

For a mocktail version substitute the tequila for 50ml/1½ fl oz of coconut water

Add all the ingredients, except the garnishes, to a blender and blend until you get an icy consistency. Wipe a cut lime around the rim of a glass and dip into sea salt. Pour the cocktail into the glass and garnish with a lime.

KOMBUCHA DAQUIRI

Serves 1
65ml/2 fl oz good quality dark rum
150ml/5 fl oz any citrus flavoured kombucha
35ml/2 tbsp honey syrup (you can buy this or just
    mix raw honey with a little warm water)

Combine all the ingredients in a cocktail shaker with ice cubes and
shake until chilled. Pour into a classic, pre-chilled cocktail glass.

KOMBUCHA MOJITO

This uses ginger and lime kombucha in place of soda, however, it does need a little extra fresh lime for the right kick!

Serves 1
2 tsp sugar
½ a fresh lime (for garnish and to taste)
2–3 sprigs of mint
50ml/1½ fl oz white rum
150ml/5 fl oz ginger and lime kombucha (see p.29)

1 Put the sugar and the juice of half a lime into the bottom of a tall straight glass. Tip: make sure the lime is at room temperature and roll it with the palm of your hand against the kitchen worktop to get the most juice out of it. Mix the sugar and lime together until the sugar has mostly dissolved.

2 Reserving one mint sprig for garnish, roll or fold the remaining mint sprigs to begin releasing their oils and put them into the bottom of the glass with the lime and sugar. Gently 'muddle' with the handle of a wooden spoon – the aim is to release the aroma and oils, not pulverize it beyond recognition!

3 Fill the glass with ice, cubed or crushed, and add the rum.

4 Lastly fill the glass to the top with ginger and lime kombucha and garnish with another sprig of mint.

LIME & GINGER KOMBUCHA ICE CREAM FLOAT

1 cup = 250 ml

1 cup cashews, soaked
½ cup young coconut meat from a Thai green coconut
½ cup agave syrup
½ cup coconut milk
½ cup lime juice
Zest of 3 limes
½ tsp vanilla extract
Pinch of salt
¼ cup coconut oil, melted
500ml lime and ginger kombucha (see p.29)
Lime zest, to garnish

1 Soak the cashew nuts for two hours in cold water. Rinse well under cold running water and drain.

2 In a high speed blender, whizz all of the ingredients except the coconut oil and kombucha, until smooth.

3 Add the coconut oil and blend again.

4 Transfer the mixture to an ice cream maker and follow the manufacturer's instructions. Alternatively you can pour the mixture into a freezer container and leave in the freezer to set for a couple of hours. After a couple of hours, use a fork to whisk up the mixture and remove any ice crystals and return to the freeze to set. Repeat this process twice every couple of hours and then store in the freezer until needed.

5 To serve, pour a long glass of chilled lime and ginger kombucha (see p. 29) and top with the coconut lime ice cream. A few shavings of lime zest make a nice garnish.

ALTERNATIVE USES

Apart from being a refreshing drink that is actually good for you, kombucha and the SCOBY itself can be useful in a number of other ways.

VINEGAR

Every so often, I deliberately neglect a batch of kombucha and leave it for months. It will come to no harm at all and will essentially turn to kombucha vinegar. Although not palatable to drink on its own, kombucha vinegar has a multitude of uses is its own right.

Kombucha vinegar is perfect for using in salad dressings in place of your standard vinegar. For a bog-standard vinaigrette dressing, mix 3 parts good quality olive oil to 1 part kombucha vinegar. This is a rough guide and can be adjusted according to taste. If you want more sharpness, just add more kombucha vinegar. Alternatively, infuse your sour kombucha with chilli and garlic for an extra zing in your dressings or marinades.

I have even been known to use kombucha vinegar on chips, although how much of the bacteria remain live will of course depend on how hot the chips are!!

A really mature vinegar is great to use for sanitising your brewing equipment in between brews without the need for harsh chemicals. The reason it is so effective is that it has a very acidic pH which is an inhospitable environment for unwanted bacteria to grow in.

TONIC

Kombucha's acidic pH can also be beneficial to our own skin, which should be slightly acidic to achieve optimal function. When skin becomes too alkaline it can be dry and sensitive. In recent years, some of the larger cosmetic brands have begun investing in research into the anti-ageing properties of kombucha and it is now listed as an active ingredient in a number of high-end, collagen-boosting, anti-ageing serums and creams. When you are brewing your own, you have an unlimited supply of this powerful raw ingredient at your fingertips. You can go as far as laying a SCOBY on your face, but this can be a little daunting (even for me!) however, some unflavoured kombucha applied with a cotton wool pad in the same way that you would a toner, can work wonders! Once the liquid dries there is no perceptible smell left and, provided you are using a mature brew (closer to starter liquid and perhaps verging on vinegar), then there will be no stickiness. I have added this to my weekly skincare regime and have to say I am regularly complimented on my complexion despite never wearing foundation.

Kombucha is also an excellent go to when you have minor skin ailments. A minor bump, graze or minor burn all benefit from a cool kombucha compress. Soak some cotton wool and apply directly to the skin. If a cooling effect is needed then replace often with fresh, cool liquid. I have been known to save any mini SCOBYs that have grown in the neck of a bottle that wasn't quite air-tight in a small jar specifically to apply to insect bites. I had an awful run last summer of getting bitten by horseflies and had a terribly painful reaction with awful swelling and pain. It was only after a week or so when it wasn't really subsiding that I thought to put one of these perfect little round discs of SCOBY directly onto the bite and sit for 20 minutes or so. I can only wish I had thought of it sooner because the relief was almost instant.

USING SCOBYS

When you have an abundance of spare cultures, offer them to friends and family so they can begin their own brewing adventure! However if they would rather drink your delicious kombucha than attempt their own, there are a few more ways you can use up your

SCOBYs (although please always keep one or two spare should anything happen to your active one). You can chop up the scoby into bite-sized chunks and feed to your animals. Chickens especially are said to absolutely love SCOBY and dogs, cats and even horses can benefit from having a small quantity mixed in with their food. Start with a very small amount and check there are no adverse effects over the coming days, then you can add in a small amount once a week as a special treat. Owners have reported glossier coats and even better mobility in arthritic older animals.

JERKY

If you are feeling particularly adventurous, you can even make jerky out of the cultures themselves. Chose a SCOBY that is about 4-5mm thick and cut into strips. Any thicker and they will be too chewy. Marinade in something of your choice, I used fermented soy sauce, honey (which helps the marinade 'stick' but also make the finished product a little sticky) and some chilli flakes. If you have a dehydrator, then put it on the lowest setting and leave it on until the pieces are completely dehydrated. If you don't have a dehydrator then you can place the pieces on a rack in the oven on the lowest setting and leave the door ajar. Remember you are looking to take the moisture out, not cook them. Once dried, store in an airtight container.

FOR THE KIDS

Getting children to drink kombucha can be a challenge. Their taste buds are programmed to prefer sweeter things and sugar and other sweeteners have permeated so many foods that encouraging a more savoury palate in children can be a real challenge. My son has suffered with constipation since birth, and I have always been keen to address this in the most

natural and gentle way possible. Whether you just want to introduce your children to kombucha or have similar ulterior motives, there are some easy ways to do this.

Most children like fizz! Whether it is the way it tickles their tongue or the unexpected burp that gives them the giggles, if you can give them some real fizz, the chances are they will be more receptive. Otherwise, you can mix a plain kombucha half and half with apple juice (as you serve, rather then stored in the bottle) as this will compliment the already apple-like taste of the kombucha.

I like to freeze some kombucha into ice-pop moulds with some chunks of fresh fruit. The novelty factor alone is enough to pique their interest and you can make the ice pops as elaborate or plain as you like. They have a sour taste that can be likened to some sour sweets that children seem to love, but without the added sugar. It is true that some of the bacteria will not survive the freezing process, however there are also some that will.

You can also make kombucha jelly. Please note that this is the only recipe in this book that is not 100% vegan. I have tried to make kombucha jelly with vegan jelly crystals, but they need boiling or very hot liquid which would destroy all of the benefits of

drinking kombucha (plus they have quite a lot of sugar). This recipe therefore requires plain gelatine powder or gelatine leaves or sheets. These you can warm until they melt and they will still set once chilled.

You can make jelly with plain kombucha, or with some added fruit purée that has been whizzed up in the blender. If you like a little more sweetness, then honey or maple syrup is a good way of adding some. Gently warm the kombucha and honey (or chosen sweetener) on the hob which can be more closely monitored that the microwave! As soon as the gelatine is combined remove from the heat, pour into a jelly mould and chill.

To turn out, run the mould under a warm tap for a few seconds, or you can freeze them and then do the same, then place the turned out jellies in the fridge to finish thawing. You don't need to consume a large quantity at all to get the benefits, and your family will have no idea that they are having such a nutritious treat!

OTHER FERMENTED DRINKS

Once you enter the world of kombucha and begin to reap the benefits, there is a whole world of fermentation available to you. One of the easiest next steps is other fermented drinks, like kefir (pronounced keh-fear or key-fur depending on where you are from or where you first hear about it!)

There are two varieties of kefir, although most will be referring to the milk variety as this is more common. There is also water kefir.

Both milk kefir and water kefir are made with grains, that aren't really grains at all. They are small jelly-like clusters of bacteria and yeast (exactly like a SCOBY but taking a different form). Milk kefir grains are creamy white or yellow in colour and feel quite firm with a protective slimy coating. Water kefir 'grains' still form in clusters but are slightly more delicate and will break apart when squeezed between your fingers. They will take on the colour of your brewing liquid, so if white sugar is used, they will be clear. I use a mixture of white sugar and rapadura (unrefined whole cane sugar) in a half and half mix which is why my 'grains' have a brownish colour. Grains multiply with each brew so can be shared amongst friends or purchased from a reliable supplier (see p.80).

In milk kefir, the lactose is converted by the grains and so many people who are dairy intolerant can consume the cultured milk. Studies have shown that consuming milk kefir can help improve lactose digestion in adults with lactose intolerance. It has a tangy and slightly fizzy taste which can be flavoured with chopped fruit. I prefer to add a tablespoon of milk kefir into a smoothie once a week or so to ensure I am getting a good range of natural probiotics from different sources.

Water kefir requires less patience and skill than kombucha brewing, as it is generally ready in 24-48 hours. It is just a mix of filtered water and sugar (varying types can be used). The grains require some mineral help, so a less refined sugar like rapadura gives them a good mineral boost, as do a few raisins or even an empty eggshell or a pinch of molasses. It can be flavoured in the same way as kombucha, but tends to build fizz more quickly too, so I add fruit and then refrigerate straight away.

First published in the United Kingdom in 2016 by
Pavilion
1 Gower Street
London
WC1E 6HD

Text © Melanie Millin, 2016
Design and layout © Pavilion Books Company
Ltd, 2016
Photography © Pavilion Books Company Ltd,
2016

ISBN: 978-1-91090-452-7

A CIP catalogue record for this book is available
from the British Library.

10 9 8 7 6 5 4 3 2 1

Reproduction by Mission, Hong Kong
Printed and bound by Toppan Leefung Printing
Ltd, China

This book can be ordered direct from the
publisher at:
www.pavilionbooks.com

To Grandma – I told you so!

ACKNOWLEDGEMENTS

Thanks to Craig for embarking on this journey with me; my best
friend, business partner, counsellor and coach, partner in crime,
golfing buddy and true love. We make an awesome team – when we
are not trying to kill each other.

To my family for always believing in me, or at least for telling me they
do even when they aren't so sure.

To Kate for doing all the jobs I am rubbish at and being organised
enough for both of us and to Debi for your unwavering support and
loan of the dehydrator.

The Ice Cream Float recipe on p.70 was kindly provided by
Deborah Durrant of Deliciously Raw (www.deliciouslyraw.co.uk).

With huge amounts of thanks to Emily Preece-Morrison for having
the vision and conviction to see Love Kombucha as a published
book. Her direction, support (and home economics skills) made
this possible.

To the team who managed to make kombucha look beautiful:
Laura Russell for her design skills, Wei Tang and her Mary Poppins
bag of props and Clare Winfield for capturing it all on camera.

To those who have mentored, questioned and encouraged us along
the way – we couldn't have done it without you.

The kombucha revolution is under way and you are all a part of it.

SUPPLIERS

www.lovekombucha.co.uk
www.happykombucha.co.uk
www.chiabia.com